International Workshop on EUV Lithography 2016

Berkeley, California, USA
13 - 16 June 2016

ISBN: 978-1-5108-4665-4

Printed from e-media with permission by:

Curran Associates, Inc.
57 Morehouse Lane
Red Hook, NY 12571

Some format issues inherent in the e-media version may also appear in this print version.

Printed by Curran Associates, Inc. (2017)

EUV Litho, Inc.
10202 Wommack Road
Austin, TX 78748
USA

Phone: (512) 462-2290
Fax: (512) 462-1898

http://euvlitho.com

Additional copies of this publication are available from:

Curran Associates, Inc.
57 Morehouse Lane
Red Hook, NY 12571 USA
Phone: 845-758-0400
Fax: 845-758-2633
Email: curran@proceedings.com
Web: www.proceedings.com

2016 International Workshop on EUV Lithography

CXRO, LBNL, Berkeley, CA, USA
June 13-16, 2016

Workshop Agenda

Monday, June 13, 2016

Short Courses

EUV Lithography .....N/A
by Vivek Bakshi (EUV Litho, Inc.), Patrick Naulleau (LBNL) and Jinho Ahn (Hanyang University)

8:30 AM -5:00 PM (Building 66 – Room 316)

Tuesday, June 14, 2016

Registration and Reception

3:30 PM- 5:00 PM	CXRO Tour (Building # 2, Fourth floor)
5:00 PM- 6:30 PM	Registration, reception & Speaker Prep (Building 54, Bay View Cafeteria)

Wednesday, June 15, 2016

8:30 AM Welcome and Introduction

Welcome to LBL
Mike Witherell, Director, LBL

Introduction to Agenda (Intro-1) .....N/A
Vivek Bakshi
EUV Litho, Inc., Austin, TX, USA

Session 1: Keynote – 1

Session Chair: Patrick Naulleau (CXRO)

EUV Lithography's Present and Future (P1) 6
Harry J. Levinson
GLOBALFOUNDRIES

EUVL Readiness for High Volume Manufacturing (P3) 8
Britt Turkot
Intel Corporation

Break (20 minutes)

Session 2: EUV Sources

Session Co-chairs: H. Mizoguchi (Gigaphoton) and Padraig Dunne (UCD)

Development of 250 W EUV Light Source For HVM Lithography (P34) (Invited) 12
H. Mizoguchi*, H. Nakarai, T. Abe, K. M Nowak, Y. Kawasuji, H. Tanaka, Y. Watanabe, T. Hori, T. Kodama, Y. Shiraishi, T. Yanagida, G. Soumagne, T. Yamada, T. Yamazaki , S. Okazaki and T. Saitou
Gigaphoton Inc. Hiratsuka facility, JAPAN

CO_2 Amplifiers to Generate > 20 kW Laser Power for Stable > 250 W Extreme Ultraviolet (EUV) Power (P33) (Invited) 11
Koji Yasui[1], Naoyuki Nakamura[2], Jun-ichi Nishimae[2], Masashi Naruse[3], and Masato Matsubara[3]
[1]Mitsubishi Electric Corporation, Head quarter, Tokyo, Japan
[2]Mitsubishi Electric Corporation, Advanced technology R&D center, Hyogo, Japan
[3]Mitsubishi Electric Corporation, Nagoya works, Nagoya, Japan

New Concepts for a High Brightness LPP EUV Source (P35) 13
Konstantin Koshelev, Alexander Vinokhodov, Mikhail Krivokoritov, Oleg Yakushev, Samir Ellwi, Denis Glushkov, Pavel Seroglazov
RnD-Isan, Moscow, Russia and ISTEQ B.V., Eindhoven, the Netherlands

Lunch 11:50 AM – 1:00 PM

Session 3: FEL based EUV Sources

Session Chairs: Alex Murokh (Radiabeam) and Erik R. Hosler (GLOBALFOUNDRIES)

Break and Group Photograph 2:00 PM (30 Minutes)

Session 4: EUV Optics

Session Chair: Regina Soufli (LLNL) and Ladislav Pina (Rigaku)

[4]*Zygo Corporation, Extreme Precision Optics, Richmond, CA 94806*

Atomic-scale investigations of formation and aging processes of EUV optics (P66) (Invited) 33
Joost W.M. Frenken
Advanced Research Center for Nanolithography (ARCNL)
Science Park 110, 1098 XG, Amsterdam, The Netherlands

Diffractive Optics for EUV Applications (P67) 34
Ryan Miyakawa, Henry Wang, Weilun Chao, and Patrick Naulleau
Center for X-ray Optics, Lawrence Berkeley National Lab, 1 Cyclotron Rd, Berkeley, CA 94720

Fabrication of EUVL Micro-field Exposure Tools with 0.5 NA (P68) 35
Luc Girard[1], Lou Marchetti[1], Jim Kennon[2], Bob Kestner[2], Regina Soufli[3], Eric Gullickson[4]
[1]*Zygo Corporation, Extreme Precision Optics (EPO), Richmond, CA 94806, USA*
[2]*Akumen Engineering, LLC. (former employees of Zygo EPO)*
[3]*Lawrence Livermore National Laboratory, 7000 East Avenue, Livermore, CA 94550*
[4]*Lawrence Berkeley National Laboratory, 1 Cyclotron Road, Berkeley, CA 94720*

Multilayer EUV Optics with Integrated IR Suppression Gratings (P69) 36
Torsten Feigl[1], Marco Perske[1], Hagen Pauer[1], Tobias Fiedler[1], Uwe Zeitner[2], Robert Leitel[2], Hans-Christoph Eckstein[2], Philipp Schleicher[2], Sven Schröder[2], Marcus Trost[2], Stefan Risse[2], Christian Laubis[3], Frank Scholze[3]
[1] *optiX fab GmbH, Hans-Knöll-Str. 6, 07745 Jena, Germany*
[2] *Fraunhofer IOF, Albert-Einstein-Str. 7, 07745 Jena, Germany*
[3] *PTB Berlin, Abbestr. 2-12, 10587 Berlin, Germany*

Adjourn: Time off for Networking

End Day 1

Thursday, June 16, 2016

Session 5: Keynote-2

Session Chair: Patrick Naulleau (CXRO)

Session 6: Mask-1

Session Co-Chairs: Ted Liang (Intel)

Break 10:00 AM (20 Minutes)

Session 7: Mask -2

Session Chair: Ken Goldberg (LBNL)

Improvement of Coherent Scattering Microscopy by applying Ptychographical Iterative Engine (P55) 21

Dong Gon Woo[1], Seongchul Hong[1], Hoon Jo[2], Whoi-Yul Kim[2], and Jinho Ahn[1]
[1]Department of Materials Science and Engineering
[2]Department of Electronics and Computer Engineering
Hanyang University, 222 Wangsimni-ro, Seongdong-gu, Seoul 133-791, Korea

Lunch 11:20 PM (90 Minutes)

Steering Committee working lunch meeting (Closed meeting)

12:50 PM Session 8: Mask -3

Session Chair: Jim Wiley (ASML)

Extreme Ultraviolet Mask Manufacturing: Challenges and Opportunities (P52) (Invited) .....N/A

Bryan Kasprowicz[1], Henry Kamberian[2]
[1]Photronics Inc., Allen, Texas, USA
[2]Photronics Boise nanoFab, Boise, Idaho, USA

Progress and Opportunities in EUV Mask Development (P53) (Invited).....19

Ted Liang
Intel Mask Operations, 3065 Bowers Avenue, Santa Clara, CA USA

EUREKA Overview (P85) (Invited) .....N/A

Patrick Naulleau
CXRO

Extending CO_2 Cryogenic Aerosol Cleaning for EUV Mask Cleaning (P57) (Invited) 23

Ivin Varghese and Charles W. Bowers
Eco-Snow Systems, RAVE N.P. Inc., 4935A Southfront Rd., Livermore, CA, USA 94551

Break 2:10 PM (20 Minutes)

Session 9: Resist -1

Session Co-Chairs: Stephen Meyers (Inpria) and Yoshi Hishiro (JSR)

EUV Radiation Chemistry Fundamentals: Novel Probing Techniques (P72) 38

Oleg Kostko, B. Xu, D. S. Slaughter, K. D. Closser, S. Bhattarai, B. Hinsberg, G. M. Wallraff, D. L . Olynick, D. G. Prendergast, P. D. Ashby, D. F. Ogletree, Y. Liu, P. Naulleau, M. Ahmed
Chemical Sciences Division, Lawrence Berkeley National Laboratory, 1 Cyclotron Rd, Berkley, CA 94720, USA

Session 10: Resist -2

Session Co-Chairs: Robert Brainard (SUNY) and Frank Ogletree (LBNL)

5:50- 7:00 PM Poster Session

7:30 -9:30 PM Dinner

Session 11: Poster Session (5:50 PM - 7:00 PM)

Session Chairs: Vivek Bakshi (EUV Litho Inc.) and Patrick Naulleau (CXRO)

Yow-Gwo Wang*[a,b], Andy Neureuther[a,b], Patrick Naulleau[b]
[a]*Department of Electrical Engineering and Computer Sciences, University of California, Berkeley, CA USA 94720;* [b]*Center for X-ray Optics, Lawrence Berkeley National Laboratory, Berkeley, CA USA 94720*

Aamod Shanker[1], AntoineWojdyla[2], Gautam Gunjala[1], Jonathan Dong[3], Markus Benk[2], Andy Neureuther[1], Kenneth Goldberg[2], Laura Waller[1]
[1]*Dept of Electrical Engineering and Computer Sciences, UC Berkeley, CA*
[2]*Center for X-Ray Optics, Lawrence Berkeley National Lab, Berkeley, CA*
[3] *D´epartement de Physique, Ecole Normale Sup´erieure, Paris 75005, France*

Yong Ju Jang[1], Jung Sik Kim[1], Seongchul Hong[2], Jinho Ahn[1,2]
[1]*Department of Nanoscale Semiconductor Engineering*
[2]*Department of Materials Science and Engineering*
Hanyang University, 222 Wangsimni-ro, Seongdong-gu, Seoul 04763, Korea

Dong Gon Woo[1], Seongchul Hong[1], Hoon Jo[2], Whoi-Yul Kim[2], and Jinho Ahn[1]
[1]*Department of Materials Science and Engineering*
[2]*Department of Electronics and Computer Engineering*
Hanyang University, 222 Wangsimni-ro, Seongdong-gu, Seoul 133-791, Korea

Bo Yu[1], Chunshui Jin[1],Chun Li[1], Shun Yao[1]
[1]*Changchun Institute of Optical, Fine Mechanics and Physics, Chinese Academy of Sciences, 3888 Dong Nanhu Road, Changchun, China, 130033*

Norbert Koster, Edwin te Sligte, Freek Molkenboer, Alex Deutz, Peter van der Walle, Pim Muilwijk, Wouter Mulckhuyse, Bastiaan Oostdijck, Christiaan Hollemans, Björn Nijland, Peter Kerkhof, Michel van Putten
TNO, Stieltjesweg 1, 2628 CK Delft, The Netherlands

[1]Kristina D. Closser, [1]David Prendergast, [2]Musa Ahmed, [1]Paul D. Ashby, [2]Oleg Kostko, [1]D. Frank Ogletree, [1]Deirdre L . Olynick, [2]D. Slaughter, [2]Bo Xu, [3]Patrick Naulleau
[1]*Molecular Foundry, Lawrence Berkeley National Laboratory*
[2]*Chemical Sciences Division, Lawrence Berkeley National Laboratory*
[3]*Center for X-ray Optics (CXRO), Lawrence Berkeley National Laboratory*

ADDITIONAL PAPERS

EUV

LITHO, INC.

Platinum Level Sponsors

ISTEQ

Gold Level Sponsors

ENERGETIQ

research instruments

radiabeam TECHNOLOGIES

TEL

RnD ISAN

Organized by

EUREKA

CXRO
THE CENTER FOR X-RAY OPTICS

EUV
LITHO, INC.

Vivek Bakshi (EUV Litho, Inc.), Chair
Patrick Naulleau (CXRO), Co-Chair

Contents

Welcome

Dear Colleagues;

I would like to welcome you to the 9th year of International Workshop on EUV Lithography (EUVL Workshop) in Berkeley, CA! At this new LBNL Campus location, this workshop continues its focus on R&D topics and we are looking forward to an excellent agenda.

This workshop has been made possible by the support of workshop sponsors, steering committee members, workshop support staff, session chairs and presenters. I would like to thank them for their contributions and for making this workshop a success. I look forward to your participation.

Best Regards

Vivek Bakshi
Chair, 2016 International Workshop on EUVL

Abstracts

(Listed by Paper number)

P1

EUV Lithography's Present and Future

Harry J. Levinson

GLOBALFOUNDRIES

After many years of uncertainty regarding its suitability for high volume manufacturing (HVM), EUV lithography now appears to be on a trajectory for use in production. Several companies have multiple EUV exposure tools that are currently being used for research and development. The transition from laboratory to pilot line provides essential learning about issues that need to be resolved in order to bring EUV lithography to full readiness for HVM. EUV lithography is beneficial even for layers which can be patterned using multiple optical exposures, because it can provide reduced cycle time. EUV lithography is particularly advantageous for contact and via layers. but applicability to layers that have large areas exposed is limited by mask blank defects. Substantial improvements in EUV source power and reliability are still required for EUV lithography to be cost equivalent to immersion triple patterning. Extension of EUV lithography to pitches below 30 nm appears to be limited by resist capability, so significant improvement in resist materials is needed to ensure the suitability of EUV lithography for future nodes. Chemically-amplified organic resists may not be capable. Extension of EUV lithography will also require higher source power in order to avoid unacceptable levels of photon shot noise induced LER. Alternatives to laser-produced plasma light sources should be considered for providing higher source power. Continuing reduction in the number and size of mask blank defects is required to avoid limited applicability of EUV lithography.

Presenting Author

Harry J. Levinson is Sr. Director of GLOBALFOUNDRIES's Strategic Lithography Technology organization and Sr. Fellow. Dr. Levinson also served for several years as the chairman of the USA Lithography Technology Working Group that participated in the generation of the lithography chapter of the International Technology Roadmap for Semiconductors. He is the author of two books, *Lithography Process Control* and *Principles of Lithography*. He holds over 60 US patents. Dr. Levinson is an SPIE Fellow, previously chaired the SPIE Publications Committee, and served on SPIE's Board of Directors. He has a BS in engineering from Cornell University and a PhD in physics from the University of Pennsylvania. His PhD thesis, titled *Resonances and Collective Effects in Photoemission*, addressed certain phenomenon involving the interactions of light and matter. For this work he received the Wayne B. Nottingham Prize in surface science.

P2

EUVL Exposure Tools for HVM: Status and Outlook

Igor Fomenkov

Cymer LLC, An ASML Company, San Diego, CA 92127, USA

NXE:3300B scanners have been operational at customer sites for two years, and in 2015 the NXE:3350B, the 4th generation EUV system, has started shipping. Today's overlay and imaging results are in line with the requirements of 7nm logic devices: matched machine overlay (MMO) to ArF immersion below 2.5 nm and full wafer CDU performance of less than 1.0nm are regularly achieved. The realization of an intensity loss-less illuminator and improvements in resist formulation are significant progress towards enabling the use of EUV technology for 5nm logic devices at full productivity. Continuous progress in defectivity reduction and in the realization of a reticle pellicle are also taking place at increased speed. Along with scanner performance, this paper describes the development of laser-produced-plasma (LPP) extreme-ultraviolet (EUV) sources for advanced lithography applications in high volume manufacturing. In this paper we discuss the most recent results from high power testing on our development systems targeted at the 250W configuration, and describe the requirements and technical challenges related to successful implementation of these technologies. Subsystem performance will be shown including Master Oscilator Power Amplifier (MOPA) Prepulse operation with high Conversion Efficiency (CE) and dose control with high energy stability enabling high die yield. We describe the most effective optimized modes of operation to control the plasma dynamics at high power while ensuring protection of collector optics. This presentation reviews the experimental results obtained on systems with a focus on the topics most critical for a 250W HVM LPP source.

Presenting Author

Igor Fomenkov is an ASML Fellow in Technology Development Group in San Diego, California. After completing a Ph.D. in Physics and Mathematics at Moscow Institute of Physics and Technology (MPTI) in 1986, he joined General Physics Institute as a senior scientist, where he worked in the field of interaction of high intensity laser radiation with matter and diagnostics of laser produced plasma. He joined Cymer in 1992 and worked on the development of high power, high reliability KrF and ArF Excimer lasers for DUV (at 248nm and 193nm) microlithography. Since 1997 he has been conducting research and development of sources for Extreme Ultraviolet Lithography at 13.5nm. He was appointed Cymer Fellow in 2003 and ASML Fellow in 2014. He has authored over 50 technical papers and holds over 100 patents in the areas of DUV and EUV light sources.

P3

EUVL Readiness for High Volume Manufacturing

Britt Turkot

Intel Corporation

Over the past two years significant strides in demonstrated source power have bolstered confidence in the viability of EUVL for insertion into HVM production. While the exposure source remains the largest contributor to downtime and availability, there has been significant overall improvement in production tools, exposure source and infrastructure to better position the technology for HVM insertion. Improvements in reticle infrastructure lag behind those of the scanner and exposure source, and predictable yield requires continued emphasis on reticles including improvements in mask blank defectivity and techniques to detect and mitigate reticle blank and pattern defects.

Presenting Author

Britt Turkot is a senior principal engineer and engineering group leader with Intel's Portland Technology Development Lithography organization where she is the EUV program manager for Intel. She has been with Intel since 1996 after receiving B.S., M.S. and Ph.D. degrees in Materials Science and Engineering from the University of Illinois at Urbana-Champaign.

P31

Influence of Pulse Duration on CO_2 Laser Produced tin Plasma by 1D Plasma Modeling

Wang Xinbing, Yao Liwei and Zuo Duluo

Wuhan National Laboratory for Optoelectronics, Huazhong University of Science & Technology, Wuhan, 430074, China

13.5 nm extreme-ultraviolet (EUV) radiation from laser-produced plasma (LPP) has been investigated extensively for application to next generation microlithography. One critical issue for LPP-EUV is the conversion efficiency (CE). The influence of CO_2 laser pulse duration has been investigated by the use of a free 1D radiation hydrodynamic code MULTI. The optimum pulse duration is determined via electron temperature and density at different time. It is found that the optimum pulse duration is 200~300 ns for a constant peak intensity of 0.5×10^{10} W/cm^2 (or 1×10^{10} W/cm^2), while the optimum pulse duration is 100~200 ns for a constant pulse energy of 850 J/cm^2. Moreover, lowering initial target density does not cause any changes in the EUV emission. Therefore, employing a long pulse, for example, 200 ns, could make the EUV lithography system more efficient, simpler, and cheaper.

Acknowledgement: Research supported by Director Fund of WNLO.

Presenting Author

Yao Liwei is the possible presenting author for this annual workshop. He is a Ph.D. candidate at Huazhong University of Science & Technology, Wuhan, China. He has started his doctorate of optical engineering at Laser and terahertz laboratory in Wuhan National Laboratory for Optoelectronics since 2012. His main research is laser produced tin-droplet plasma simulation.

Wang Xinbing is the possible presenting author. He is the professor in Huazhong University of Science & Technology, Wuhan, China. His main research is laser produced tin-droplet plasma simulation.

P32

Laboratory Soft X-ray Tomography with a Simple Robust Laser Plasma Light Source

F. O'Reilly[1,2], G. Wielgoszewski[2], J. Howard[2], F. McGrath[2], R. Byrne[2], A. Mahon[2], O. Hammad[2], T. McEnroe[2], T. McCormack[1], G. O'Sullivan[1], E. Sokell[1], P. Dunne[1], N. Kennedy[1], K. Fahy[2], P. Sheridan[2]

1 University College Dublin, School of Physics, Dublin, Ireland
2 SiriusXT Ltd, Science Centre North, Belfield, Ireland

Great progress has been made over the last decade in developing cryogenic soft x-ray tomography (SXT) as an imaging technique using synchrotron-based microscopes. SXT exploits the natural contrast between carbon and water that results from the different energies of the k-shell absorption edges in carbon and oxygen. SXT operates in the spectral region between 2.3 & 4.4 nm, the "water window".

Workflows and data analysis have improved, allowing researchers, who are not expert in synchrotron use to access the technique. In addition, significant expertise has been developed in correlating SXT and fluorescence microscopy data. Here we report on the development of a new lab-based microscope, using a laser-produced plasma source, which aims to deliver synchrotron performance in a system that will turn SXT into an affordable and efficient laboratory tool. We show data on source performance and images of test samples.

Presenting Author

P33

CO_2 Amplifiers to Generate > 20 kW Laser Power for Stable > 250 W Extreme Ultraviolet (EUV) Power

Koji Yasui[1], Naoyuki Nakamura[2], Jun-ichi Nishimae[2], Masashi Naruse[3], and Masato Matsubara[3]

[1]*Mitsubishi Electric Corporation, Head quarter, Tokyo, Japan*
[2]*Mitsubishi Electric Corporation, Advanced technology R&D center, Hyogo, Japan*
[3]*Mitsubishi Electric Corporation, Nagoya works, Nagoya, Japan*

We have developed transverse-gas-flow CO_2 lasers to generate > 20 kW laser powers by amplifying laser powers from oscillators developed by Gigaphoton Inc[1)]. EUV powers of > 250W could be generated by using plasma generation schemes by Gigaphoton Inc[1)] with state-of-the-art pre-pulse technology by using CO_2 laser powers of >20 kW. After confirming the generation of > 25 kW by using experimental proto-type, we are now trying to prove better performances based on commercially available product versions with smaller footprints compared with conventional amplifiers. At the workshop, to cope with requirements for further enhancements of laser powers with better efficiency, we are also going to discuss about estimations based on both theoretical and experimental results.

1) Hakaru Mizoguchi, et al.:" Performance of new high-power HVM LPP-EUV source", Proc. SPIE 9776,(2016) [9776-20]

Presenting Author

Koji Yasui received B.S. and Ph. D. degrees from the University of Tokyo in 1982 and 1989 respectively. He was a visiting scientist at the Stanford University in 1989. He joined Mitsubishi Electric Corporation in 1982, where he has developed high-power CO_2 lasers, high-power solid-state lasers, high-power green lasers, high-power UV lasers and laser processing machines using those laser sources. He is now in charge of laser technology, EDM technology, CNC technology and e-beam technology and related businesses.

P34

Development of 250 W EUV Light Source For HVM Lithography

H. Mizoguchi*, H. Nakarai, T. Abe, K. M Nowak, Y. Kawasuji, H. Tanaka, Y. Watanabe, T. Hori, T. Kodama, Y. Shiraishi, T. Yanagida, G. Soumagne, T. Yamada, T. Yamazaki , S. Okazaki and T. Saitou

Gigaphoton Inc. Hiratsuka facility, JAPAN

We have been developing CO_2-Sn-LPP EUV light source which is the most promising solution as the 13.5nm high power light source for HVM EUVL. Unique and original technologies such as; combination of pulsed CO_2 laser and Sn droplets, dual wavelength laser pulses shooting and mitigation with magnetic field have been developed in Gigaphoton Inc.. We have reported engineering data from our resent test such around 118W average clean power, CE=3.7%, with 100kHz operation and other data [1)]. We have already finished preparation of higher average power CO_2 laser more than 20kW at output power cooperate with Mitsubishi electric cooperation[2)]. Recently we have reported 108W, continuous operation with 50% duty cycle during 24hours [3)].cFurther improvements are underway, we will report the latest data: (1) more than 200 W open loop level operation condition (2) Stable 150W feedback loop continuous operation during more than 3 days with around 4% CE with 20 micron droplet and magnetic mitigation. Also we will report the latest data of Pilot 250 W EUV source system.

1) Hakaru Mizoguchi, et. al., "Sub-hundred Watt operation demonstration of HVM LPP-EUV source," Proc. SPIE 9048, (2014)
2) Yoichi Tanino et.al., "A Driver CO2 Laser Using Transverse-flow CO2 Laser Amplifiers," EUV Symposium 2013, (Toyama)
3) Hakaru Mizoguchi, et al., " Performance of new high-power HVM LPP-EUV source", Proc. SPIE 9776 (2016) [9776-20]

Presenting Author

Hakaru Mizoguchi is Executive Vice President and CTO of Gigaphoton Inc.

He is member of The International Society of Optical Engineering, The Laser Society of Japan and The Japan Society of Applied Physics. He received a diplomat degree in plasma diagnostics field from the Kyushu university, Fukuoka, Japan in 1982 and join Komatsu Ltd. He joined CO2 laser development program in Komatsu for 6 years. Since 1990 he concentrated on KrF, ArF excimer laser and F2 laser research and development for lithography application. He was general manager of research division in Komatsu Ltd. until 1999. He got Dr. degree in high power excimer laser field from Kyushu university in 1994. He was one of the founders of Gigaphoton Inc. in 2000. From 2002 to 2010 he organized EUV research group in EUVA program. Now he is promoting EUV light source product development with present position.

P35

New Concepts for a High Brightness LPP EUV Source

Konstantin Koshelev, Alexander Vinokhodov, Mikhail Krivokoritov, Oleg Yakushev, Samir Ellwi, Denis Glushkov, Pavel Seroglazov

RnD-Isan, Moscow, Russia
ISTEQ B.V., Eindhoven, the Netherlands

ISTEQ/RnD-ISAN have significant experience in the development of DPP and LPP EUV light sources. For the last few years we have been focused on the development of an EUV source for mask and wafer inspection. The critical parameters for an actinic source are high brightness, dose stability, long lifetime and compact size. We propose two advanced LPP approaches, already experimentally demonstrated, which can be used for manufacturing a compact high-brightness EUV source.

1) For a conventional droplet target scheme we propose to use low melting temperature tin alloy as a fuel, which leads to a radical improvement in droplet generator performance. Experimental data shows optimal source conversion efficiency with minimal debris and high stability.
2) A new approach, which we have developed, is the "no debris" concept based on the usage of liquid lithium jet as a target placed inside a compact closed volume with self-cleaning input and output windows. This concept provides a number of significant advantages, providing higher EUV dose stability and longer optics lifetime. This makes the use of Lithium as a fuel for EUV sources highly attractive. Experimental data will be presented.

Both approaches are currently in the development phase. As the project reaches the stage where potential customer participation is critical, we would like to present our work.

Presenting Author

Dr. Samir Ellwi currently holds the position of Non-Executive Managing Director at ISTEQ B.V., a company which specializes in the development and manufacturing of light sources ranging from soft X-rays to infrared. He is the co-founder and CEO of ALSPhotonics, a consultancy company concentrating on light sources and their applications. He has more than 20 years experience in laser, laser applications and light sources. He holds a PhD from University of Essex/UK "X-ray and Optical Studies of Dense Plasmas". Prior to ISTEQ, he worked as a Managing Director at Adlyte/Switzerland, a company specializing in the development of EUV light sources. Previously he was Vice President at Powerlase/UK and a member of the executive management team. He worked as a senior scientist in the research group at ASML.

P36

Stable Droplet Generator for High brightness LPP EUV Source

Konstantin Koshelev[1,2], Alexander Vinokhodov[1], Mikhail Krivokorytov[1], Yuri Sidelnikov[2], Oleg Yakushev[1], Denis Glushkov[3], Pavel Seroglazov[3] , Samir Ellwi[3]

1. RnD-ISAN/EUV Labs, Troitsk, 142190 Russia
2. Institute for Spectroscopy RAS, Troitsk, 142090 Russia
3. ISTEQ, 5656 AG Eindhoven

The EUV source has the potential to be used for mask inspection. Mask inspection requires an EUV source with less power but more brightness and higher pulse-to-pulse EUV energy and spatial stability. It was shown that laser produced plasma based on tin droplets is suitable for this task due to a small source size defined by droplet size. In order to achieve the requirements of energy and spatial stability, it is first necessary to have a high stability droplet generator.

In this work we present the design of droplet generator, which operates on the principle of excited Rayleigh breakup of liquid jet. The parameters of best operation mode are the following: droplet diameter of 46 μm, repetition rate 40 kHz, droplet-to-droplet position stability ~ 1% (of droplet diameter) at a distance 40 mm from the nozzle and time of operation - 2 hours. In this work we show that such a droplet generator can be used for producing a laser plasma source with properties suitable for inspection tasks.

Presenting Author

Dr. Samir Ellwi currently holds the position of Non-Executive Managing Director at ISTEQ B.V., a company which specializes in the development and manufacturing of light sources ranging from soft X-rays to infrared. He is the co-founder and CEO of ALSPhotonics, a consultancy company concentrating on light sources and their applications. He has more than 20 years of experience in laser, laser applications and light sources. He holds a PhD from University of Essex/UK "X-ray and Optical Studies of Dense Plasmas". Prior to ISTEQ, he worked as a Managing Director at Adlyte/Switzerland, a company specializing in the development of EUV light sources. Previously he was Vice President at Powerlase/UK and a member of the executive management team. He worked as a senior scientist in the research group at ASML.

P41

Free-electron Lasers: Beyond EUV Lithography Insertion

Erik R. Hosler, Obert R. Wood II

GLOBALFOUNDRIES, 400 Stone Break Road Extension, Malta, NY 12020

Recent increases in the power and availability of laser-produced plasma sources have all but eliminated the uncertainty concerning the use of extreme-ultraviolet (EUV) lithography in high-volume manufacturing. Technical feasibility studies are being replaced by questions related to technology insertion (node and process layers) and extendibility. Given the persistent delay in the transition to manufacturing, the value of EUV single exposure has been progressively diluted with each missed insertion target and increased the required EUV source power beyond 250 W. Considering future patterning and productivity requirements at the 5 nm technology node and beyond, sources powers of 500-1000 W at a reduced operational cost per wafer may be required.

A free-electron laser (FEL) EUV source offers a cost effective, single-source alternative for powering a manufacturing fab's entire EUV lithography module. Multiple FEL emission and accelerator architectures have been proposed, offering a variety of configurations capable of achieving the prerequisites for use with semiconductor manufacturing. However, each configurational design and component choice can impact the efficiency and capabilities of a fab integrated FEL, while the rapid development of advanced accelerator technology could substantially reduce a future light source facility capital/operational cost and size. Architectural options and recent progress in accelerator and FEL technology relevant to high-power applications are reviewed in the context of a manufacturing program with respect to potential benefits and pitfalls.

Presenting Author

Erik Hosler is a Principal Engineer in the Strategic Lithography Technology Department at GLOBALFOUNDRIES, focusing on emerging lithography and tool innovations, including disruptive technologies. He earned his Ph.D. from the University of California at Berkeley in 2013 in Physical Chemistry, studying ultrafast chemical dynamics with Stephen R. Leone. Since joining GLOBALFOUNDRIES, he has been involved in the EUV source development, including the evaluation of free-electron lasers for use in the semiconductor manufacturing.

P42

A Path Towards an FEL-based High-power EUV Source

Tor Raubenheimer

SLAC National Accelerator Laboratory (SLAC)

High power FEL's based on modern superconducting RF technology offer the potential to generate 10's of kW in the EUV. Multiple approaches towards this goal exist including energy-recovery linacs and single-pass linacs driving SASE or high-efficiency FEL systems. All of these accelerators would be large complex systems with differing levels of demonstration. This paper will outline the different approaches, focusing on the single-pass linacs and describe the technical challenges as well as the timescales and risks.

Presenting Author

Tor Raubenheimer is a professor at the SLAC National Accelerator Laboratory (SLAC) and Stanford University. He is an expert in accelerator physics, design issues in high energy linear accelerators, ion/beam-plasma instabilities in rings and linacs, and effects during bunch length compression. Since 2011, Prof. Raubenheimer has been leading the accelerator physics design for the LCLS-II, a future high power X-Ray Free Electron Laser based on a 4 GeV Superconducting RF linac. From 2007 through 2011, Prof. Raubenheimer was Division Director for the SLAC Accelerator Research Division where he helped launch the SLAC FACET Test Facility as well as SLAC LHC Accelerator Research (LARP) and SLAC Muon Accelerator (MAP) R&D efforts. Between 1997 and 2007, he was the head of Accelerator Physics for the Next Linear Collider project and then head of the International Linear Collider Division at SLAC. Prof. Raubenheimer joined the SLAC faculty in 1997 and has been a full professor since 2007. He has authored over 50 refereed journal articles and 300 conference papers. He is a fellow of the American Physical Society and received the American Physical Society's Division of Beam Physics Dissertation Award as well as the U.S. Particle Accelerator School Prize for Achievement in Accelerator Physics and Technology.

P43

Design and Development of a 10-kW Class EUV-FEL Project in Japan

Ryukou Kato

High Energy Accelerator Research Organization (KEK)
Tsukuba, Ibaraki, 305-0801 Japan

Laser is one of the greatest inventions in the 20th century. Its wavelength is, however, restricted within the region from near infrared to vacuum ultraviolet since it depends on the gain medium and the efficient mirror. Self-amplified spontaneous emission (SASE) using the high-gain single-pass free-electron laser (FEL) configuration without mirrors is one of promising approaches to realize short wavelength lasers. On the other hand, an energy recovery linac (ERL) based on superconducting technologies realizes a high-quality, high-average power electron beam. A combination of FEL and ERL is a possible candidate for high power EUV light source for lithography, which is awaited by the semiconductor manufacturing industry. A consortium of KEK, JAEA, other laboratories and universities, and several companies in Japan is investigating a EUV-FEL based on the 800 MeV ERL operating at the wavelength of 13.5 nm with an average power more than 10 kW. We will present recent progress of the EUV-FEL design work and results of FEL simulations.

Presenting Author

P51

Eigenmode Analysis of Electromagnetic Fields in Binary EUV Masks

Michael Yeung[1], Eytan Barouch[2] and Hye-Keun Oh[3]

[1]*Fastlitho, 123 E. San Carlos Street, #251, San Jose, CA 95112*
[2]*Boston University, 15 St. Mary's Street, Boston, MA 02215*
[3]*Hanyang University, Ansan, Gyeonggi 426-791, Republic of Korea*

As feature size is reduced, the dimensions of the openings in the absorber layer of a binary EUV mask can be not much larger than a wavelength of light. In this regime, light propagation through the absorber openings cannot be described accurately by geometrical or physical optics. Instead, rigorous electromagnetic theory must be used.

In this paper, the electromagnetic fields inside binary EUV masks are analyzed by decomposing them into exact eigenmodes. Each of the dominant eigenmodes is then studied in terms of its propagation characteristics and how it interacts with the multilayered mirror to produce a reflected wave. The result of this study reveals not only that different eigenmodes are responsible for different aspects of the aerial image on the wafer and that the problems of shadowing and mask-side non-telecentricity become less serious as the feature size is reduced, but also that there is a built-in attenuating phase-shifting mask effect in all binary EUV masks, regardless of feature size, which can be utilized to improve aerial-image
contrast.

Presenting Author

Michael Yeung received his doctorate in EECS from U.C. Berkeley in 1995. He has worked at Intel as an optical lithographer and has taught at Boston University for ten years where his research interest was in computational electromagnetics. In 2006 he began working for himself developing electromagnetic simulation software for the microchip industry, as well as continuing to do research in advanced lithography.

P53

Progress and Opportunities in EUV Mask Development

Ted Liang

Intel Mask Operations, 3065 Bowers Avenue, Santa Clara, CA USA

Significant progress toward HVM readiness has been made in EUV mask fabrication and quality control that enabled the demonstration of technological viability of EUVL for production as well as wafer yield printed with defect free masks. However, to be fully ready for high-volume manufacturing, major improvements are still needed in mask materials, fabrication processes, defect inspection and disposition metrology and mask protection with a pellicle during use in scanners. In particular, pellicle and mask inspection are two critical areas of development in the overall EUV mask infrastructure and will be the topics of discussion in this presentation.

In this presentation, first described are the importance and general technology requirements of EUV pellicle and mask pattern inspection, followed by a review of the current status and remaining challenges. Then the opportunities in pellicle materials development and innovation will be discussed.

Presenting Author

P54

Off-axis Aberration Estimation in an EUV Microscope using Natural Speckle

Aamod Shanker[1], AntoineWojdyla[2], Gautam Gunjala[1], Jonathan Dong[3], Markus Benk[2], Andy Neureuther[1], Kenneth Goldberg[2], Laura Waller[1]

[1]Dept of Electrical Engineering and Computer Sciences, University of California, Berkeley, CA
[2]Center for X-Ray Optics, Lawrence Berkeley National Lab, Berkeley, CA
[3] D´epartement de Physique, Ecole Normale Sup´erieure, Paris 75005, France

Surface roughness on a flat object causes natural speckle when imaged by an extreme ultraviolet (EUV) microscope under sufficient coherence. Using a phase-to-intensity transfer function theory, direct estimation of aberrations from the spectrum of the speckle intensity is demonstrated for various illumination angles.

Acknowledgements

The LBNL EUV program is supported by Eureka, and initial funding for SHARP was from SEMATECH. The Advanced Light Source is supported by the Director, Office of Science, Office of Basic Energy Sciences, of the U.S. Department of Energy under Contract No. DE-AC02-05CH11231. UC Berkeley support by IMPACT+ group of companies - Applied Materials, ARM, ASML, Global Foundries, IBM, Intel, KLA-Tencor, Marvell Technology, Mentor Graphics, Panoramic Tech, Photronics, Qualcomm, San-Disk and Tokyo Electron.

Presenting Author

Aamod is a final year graduate student at the University of California, Berkeley, where he is researching phase imaging methods with applications in microscopy and lithography. His undergraduate degree was from the Indian Institute of Technology, Kharagpur, India in 2011.

P55

Improvement of Coherent Scattering Microscopy by applying Ptychographical Iterative Engine

Dong Gon Woo[1], Seongchul Hong[1], Hoon Jo[2], Whoi-Yul Kim[2], and Jinho Ahn[1]

[1]*Department of Materials Science and Engineering*
[2]*Department of Electronics and Computer Engineering*
Hanyang University, 222 Wangsimni-ro, Seongdong-gu, Seoul 133-791, Korea

We have been developing an actinic metrology tool which is called a Coherent Scattering Microscopy (CSM). CSM can observe mask pattern, but also can extract aerial image through feeding the illumination condition into the image reconstruction algorithm. Recently, we adopted the Ptychographic Iterative Engine (PIE) into CSM in order to enlarge the inspection area. PIE is the recently developed phase retrieval algorithm of Coherent Diffractive Imaging (CDI) which has been demonstrated successfully in the field of X-ray wavelengths. We adopted PIE for the inspection of EUV mask and EUV pellicle to overcome the limit of small field of view (FOV) of CSM.

We verified the performance of PIE by comparing the reconstructed images of the 128 nm L/S pattern with the image reconstructed by other phase retrieval algorithm. Compared to previous CDI, such as Error Reduction Algorithm (ERA) and Hybrid Input-Output (HIO) algorithm, PIE shows larger FOV and improved convergence speed. This results show the possibility of PIE as an imaging algorithm in EUV actinic technology. We also developed modified PIE (e.g., extended PIE (ePIE) and position correcting PIE (pcPIE)) which can compensate the instability of inspection source and relative position error between the series of diffraction pattern which are inevitable. We will show improved performance of CSM resulted from applying the PIE through the presentation.

Presenting Author

Dong Gon Woo is a graduate student under prof. Jinho Ahn in Hanyang University, South Korea.

P56

Improving SRAF margin and imaging performance by using PSM in EUVL

Yong Ju Jang[1], Jung Sik Kim[1], Seongchul Hong[2], Jinho Ahn[1,2]

[1]*Department of Nanoscale Semiconductor Engineering*
[2]*Department of Materials Science and Engineering*
Hanyang University, 222 Wangsimni-ro, Seongdong-gu, Seoul 04763, Korea

Sub-resolution assist feature (SRAF) is considered in extreme ultraviolet lithography (EUVL) to increase a common depth of focus (DOF) between a dense and an isolated pattern for printing 7 nm node at 0.33NA. However, adopting SRAF in EUVL has some issues: too small SRAF pattern is difficult to fabricate and has no optical proximity correction effect while too large SRAF will be printed. Therefore, it is beneficial to extend the limit of non-printing SRAF width. In this study, attenuated phase shift mask (PSM) having 6% reflectivity at dark region and a 180° phase shift at 13.5 nm wavelength is suggested to maximize the non-printing SRAF width. Aerial image and photoresist patterning simulation were performed using PROLITH X5.1 of KLA-Tencor to compare printing performance of binary intensity mask (BIM) and the PSM. PSM allows a larger size window of SRAF, which is a big advantage in mask manufacturing. The common DOF is also enlarged due to the increased SRAF width. Additionally, critical dimension uniformity and line edge roughness of PSM with SRAF are improved.

Presenting Author

Yong Ju Jang is a graduate student under prof. Jinho Ahn in Hanyang University, South Korea.

P57

Extending CO_2 Cryogenic Aerosol Cleaning for EUV Mask Cleaning

Ivin Varghese and Charles W. Bowers

Eco-Snow Systems, RAVE N.P. Inc., 4935A Southfront Rd., Livermore, CA, USA 94551

Cryogenic CO_2 aerosol cleaning is a dry, chemically-inert and residue-free process being implemented in production environments of optical lithography masks both in the mask shops and wafer fab. It is an effective cleaning option for removal of printable soft defects and repair debris down to the 50 nm printability specification. This technique utilizes CO_2 clusters formed by sudden expansion of liquid from high to almost atmospheric pressure through an optimally designed nozzle orifice. These CO_2 clusters are directed on to the soft defects or repair debris for momentum transfer and subsequent damage-free removal from the mask substrate. No degradation of the mask properties after CO_2 processing, i.e., no critical dimension (CD) change, no transmission/phase losses, or chemical residue that leads to haze formation, implies no restriction on number of mask CO_2 cleaning cycles.

In this paper, we report a) successful removal of soft defects and Post-RAVE repair debris without damage to the fragile SRAF features on optical masks, b) 50 CO_2 cleaning cycles of Ruthenium film on the EUV Front-side demonstrating no Ru film degradation, d) successful removal of micron-sized e-chuck defects on backside of EUV masks. In conclusion, CO_2 cryogenic aerosol cleaning can be extended to cleaning of extreme ultraviolet (EUV) masks.

Presenting Author

Ivin Varghese is a Senior R&D Scientist at, ECO-SNOW SYSTEMS, a division of RAVE N.P., Inc. in Livermore, CA.

P58

EUV Pellicle and Mask Metrology for High Volume Manufacturing

Rupert C. C. Perera

EUV Tech Inc., 2840 Howe Road, Suite A, Martinez CA, 94553 USA

Extreme Ultraviolet (EUV) Lithography is poised to enter high volume manufacturing (HVM) in the near future. One of the principal challenges in the EUVL implementation for high volume manufacturing is the availability of necessary clean at wavelength metrology tools. Since the company's inception in 1999, EUV Tech has pioneered the development of EUV Metrology tools.

EUV Tech recently developed a EUV Pellicle inspection tool to measure EUV pellicle transmission and thermal absorption. Recent results from measuring a variety of candidate EUV pellicles will be shown to highlight the measurement performance of the tool.

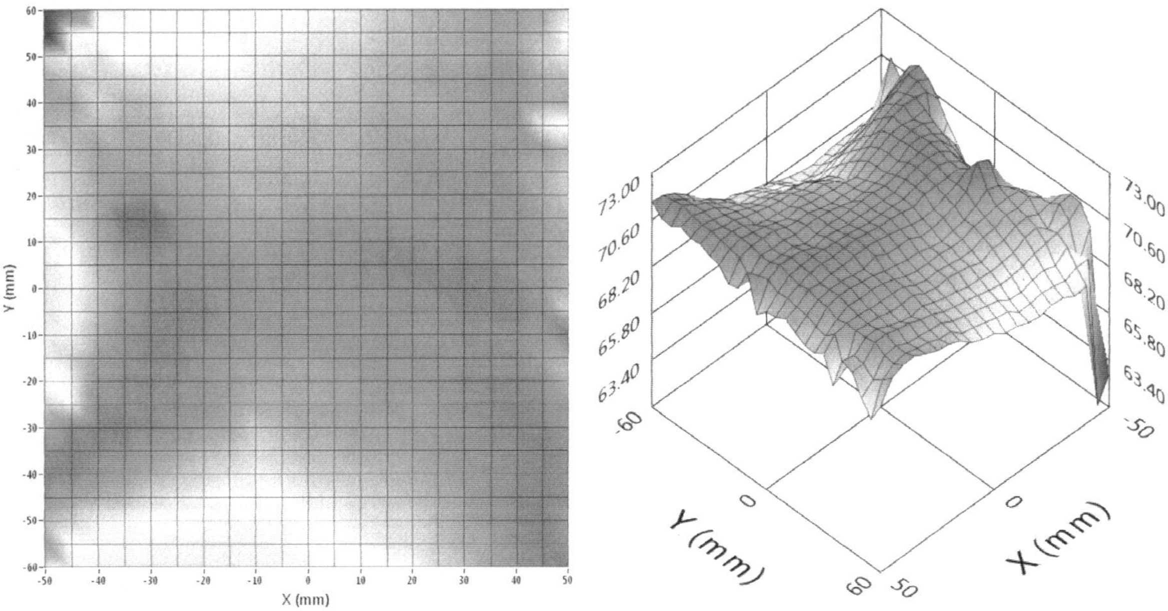

Fig. 1 Mapping of Pellicle EUVT333

EUV Reflectometry provides key measurement information for the qualification of a photomask for use in a EUV Scanner. The data is useful for a variety of users across the EUV photomask development lifecycle.

EUV Tech recently delivered an HVM EUV Reflectometer which provides at-wavelength EUV metrology of a photomask with a high precision beamline and an ultra-clean reticle transfer system. This tool is currently in use at a production mask shop. This paper will discuss the measurement performance and data output of the tool along with some uses cases within the photomask development lifecycle.

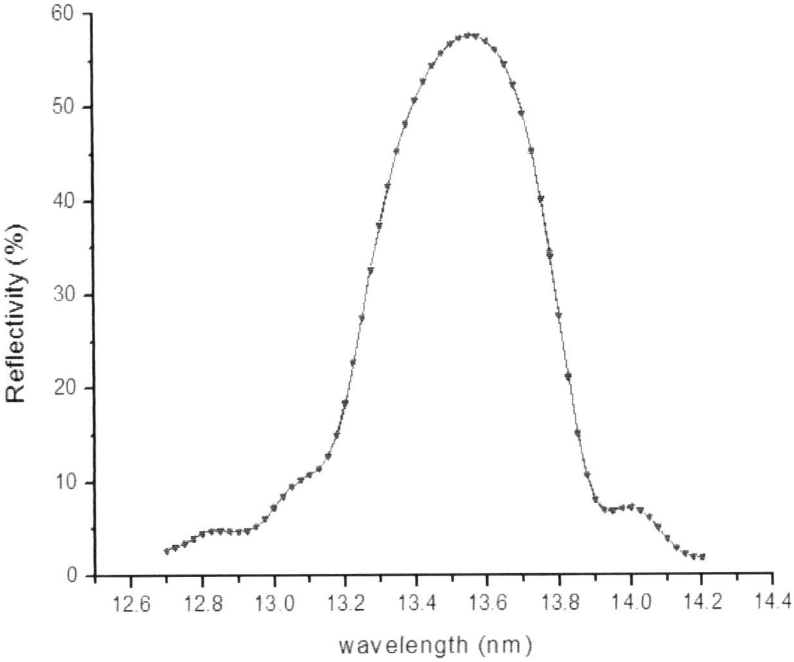

Fig. 2 EUV Multilayer Curve

This paper will also discuss, EUV Tech's R&D program and roadmap to minimize particle adders in our EUV Reflectometer along with the ongoing effort to minimize the reflectivity and wavelength, precision and accuracy required to qualify the EUV masks for current and future processing nodes.

Presenting Author

P59

Near Wavelength Limited, 15nm Spatial Resolution, Ptychographic Imaging using a 13.5nm Tabletop High Harmonic Light Source

Henry Kapteyn

KMLabs Inc., 1855 S. 57th Court, Boulder, CO 80301 USA

We have combined a spatially coherent high harmonic light source with ptychographic coherent diffractive imaging to implement high contrast, high numerical aperture, reflection and transmission mode tabletop microscopes. We made advances in two areas due to the excellent stability of the KMLabs engineered XUUS high harmonic light source. First, we implemented near-wavelength spatial resolution imaging at a wavelength of 13.5nm, achieving a lateral spatial resolution of 15nm, and <5Å axial resolution. This is the highest demonstrated resolution for a full-field tabletop microscope using any light source, and has great potential for further improvements in both spatial resolution and speed. Second, we implemented high-resolution imaging of buried interfaces, with elemental and chemical specificity, in 2+1 dimensions. A damascene-style sample was coated with 100nm thick layer of aluminum, which is opaque to visible light and thick enough that neither optical microscopy, SEM, nor AFM can access the buried interface. Our tabletop EUV microscope can image the buried structures, non-destructively, and detect when interdiffusion of materials is occuring at the interface. Finally, we also demonstrated that high harmonics can sensitively measure the elastic properties of very thin films.

Presenting Author

Dr. Henry Kapteyn is CEO of KMLabs, having worked with to commercialize ultrafast laser and coherent short wavelength source technologies. He received his Ph.D. degree from UC Berkeley, and is a Fellow of the Optical Society of America, the American Physical Society, and the AAAS. He was elected to the National Academy of Sciences in 2013, and shared the 2009 Ahmed Zewail Award of the American Chemical Society, the 2010 Schawlow Prize of the American Physical Society, and the 2010 R.W. Wood Prize of the Optical Society of America.

P61

EUV Lithography High-NA Scanner for Sub 8 nm Resolution

Jan van Schoot[1], Eelco van Setten[1], Gerardo Bottiglieri[1], Kars Troost[1], Sascha Migura[2], Jens-Timo Neumann[2], Bernhard Kneer[2], Winfried Kaiser[2]

[1]*ASML, De Run 6501, 5504 DR Veldhoven, Netherlands*

[2]*Carl Zeiss SMT GmbH, Rudolf-Eber-Straße 2, 73447 Oberkochen, Germany*

EUV lithography for resolutions at 8 nm half pitch and below requires the numerical aperture (NA) of the projection lens to be significantly larger than the current state-of-the-art 0.33NA. In order to be economically viable, a throughput above 100 wafers per hour is needed. As a result of the increased NA, the incidence angles of the light rays at the reticle increase significantly. Consequently the shadowing deteriorates the aerial image contrast to unacceptably low values.

As shown before [1], the only solution to reduce the angular range at the reticle is to increase the magnification in the scanning direction. Simulations show that we have to double the magnification to 8x in order to overcome the shadowing effects. This results into an anamorphic step and scan system, with which we can print fields that are half the size of the current full field, where the main assumption is that we keep the current 6" mask size. By increasing the transmission of the optics and by increasing the acceleration of the wafer- and reticle stage we can enable a throughput in excess of 150 wafers per hour, making this an economically viable lithography solution. In this paper we will show the impact on the several system components and how to optimize for throughput, CDU and overlay. Special attention will be given to the imaging aspects of the High-NA system.

[1] J.B.P van Schoot, K. van Ingen Schenau, C. Valentin and S. Migura, "EUV lithography scanner for sub-8nm resolution," Proc. SPIE **9422**, (2015).

Presenting Author

Jan B.P. van Schoot, PhD, joined ASML in 1996. In 1997 he became Project Leader for the Application of the first 5500/500 scanner as well as its successors up to the 5500/750. In 2001 he became Product Development Manager of Imaging Products (DoseMapper, Customized Illumination). Since 2007 he is Senior Principal Architect in the department of System Engineering. He was responsible for the Optical Columns of the NXE:3100 and NXE:3300 EUV systems. Currently he is the Study Leader of the High-NA EUV system Van Schoot studied Electrical Engineering at the Twente University of Technology. He received his PhD in Physics on the subject of Optical Waveguide Devices. He holds over 20 patents in the field of optical lithography.

P62

Multilayer Development for EUV Lithography in CIOMP

Bo Yu[1], Chunshui Jin[1], Chun Li[1], Shun Yao[1]

[1]Changchun Institute of Optical, Fine Mechanics and Physics, Chinese Academy of Sciences, 3888 Dong Nanhu Road, Changchun, China, 130033

We present an overview of recent development of multilayer coatings for EUV Lithography in CIOMP. The coating process used is magnetron sputtering. The reflectance of the coatings is typically around 69%. An inversion method based on a genetic algorithm has been developed to control the lateral thickness gradients of Mo/Si multilayer deposited on curved substrates. For the coating of projection optics, non-compensable added figure error is below 0.1 nm rms, and the wavelength uniformity across each mirror surface is within 0.2% P-V. To meet the wide angular bandpass requirement of illumination optics, the process of depth graded multilayer coatings has also been developed.

Presenting Author

Bo Yu is a Research Assistant in State Key Laboratory of Applied Optics (SKLAO), Changchun Institute of Optics, Fine Mechanics and Physics (CIOMP), Chinese Academy of Sciences (CAS), China. His main research interests are EUV/SXR multilayer coatings. He is also a PhD student of Prof. Jin Chun-shui who has been working on short-wavelength optics for about 30 years, especially on thin films, EUV optics, optical testing and integration.

P63

The Development of Extreme Ultraviolet Lithography (EUVL) Objective System in China

Chun-shui Jin[1], Dong-mei Ma[1], Xiang-zhao Wang[2], Song Hu[3], Chang-qing Xie[4], Yan-qiu Li[5], Qi Wang[6], Pei-xiang Lu[7], Li-ping Wang[1]

[1]Changchun Institute of Optical, Fine Mechanics and Physics, Chinese Academy of Sciences, 3888 Dong Nanhu Road, Changchun, China, 130033

[2]Shanghai Institute of Optics and Fine Mechanics, 390 Qinghe Road, Shanghai, China, 201800

[3]Institute of Optics and Electronics, Chinese Academy of Sciences, Box 350, Shuangliu, Chengdu, China, 610209

[4]Institute of Microelectronics of Chinese Academy of Sciences, 3 Beitucheng West Road, Beijing, China, 100029

[5]Beijing Institute of Technology, 5 South Zhongguancun Street, Beijing, China, 100081

[6]Harbin Institute of Technology, 92 West Dazhi Street, Harbin, China, 150001

[7]Huazhong University of Science & Technology, Luoyu Road 1037, Wuhan, China, 430074

The research of extreme ultraviolet lithography (EUVL) of China started relatively late at 1990s. As the core of the EUVL system, the objective is one of the most advanced and precise imaging systems, facing variety of challenges in optics, mechanics and manufacturing. Since 2009, our EUVL team has focused on the development of a two-mirror objective with small exposure filed and high NA (NA=0.3). The main researches range from high-accuracy optical testing and fabrication, EUV multilayer films, semi-kinematic mount, six-DOF precise adjustment platform to objective alignment based on our homemade point diffraction interferometer (PDI) etc. The first high NA EUVL objective with small field of view (FOV) has been accomplished late 2015. The testing result indicates that the final wavefront errors after alignment are less than 0.8nmRMS, reaching near-diffraction-limited over the 300×500μm rectangular exposure field. The integration of the whole exposure apparatus has been done and the exposure process experiments are in full swing now. This paper will present a review of the EUVL systems, especially the optical systems development in China.

Presenting Author

Dr. Chun-shui Jin is a professor at Changchun Institute of Optical, Fine Mechanics and Physics, Chinses Academy of Sciences (CIOMP, CAS). He is also one of the members of the panel of the National Sciences and Technology Major Project (NSTMP). He received his B.Sc. from Zhejiang University in 1987, and Ph.D. from CIOMP in 2003 respectively. He has been working in CIOMP since 1990.

Since 1987, his main research has always focused on short wavelength optics, including DUV/EUV multilayer films, high accuracy optical testing and fabrication, optical system integration etc. In 2003, his group accomplished the first 10× EUV micro-exposure tool in China and achieved the 250 nm dense L/S pattern. In 2008, as the director of one program of the NSTMP, Dr. Jin with his group started the key technical research on EUV lithography, focusing on the development of a 0.3 NA, two-asphere EUV static exposure system, and finished the integration of the exposure system in 2015.

P64

Multilayer coatings for the first Micro-Exposure Tools with NA=0.5

Regina Soufli[1], Jeff Robinson[1], Eberhard Spiller[2], Monica Fernández-Perea[1], Eric Gullikson[3], Luc Girard[4], Lou Marchetti[4], John Kincade[4]

[1]*Lawrence Livermore National Laboratory, Livermore, CA 94550*
[2]*Spiller X-ray Optics, Livermore, CA 94550*
[3]*Lawrence Berkeley National Laboratory, Berkeley, CA 94720*
[4]*Zygo Corporation, Extreme Precision Optics, Richmond, CA 94806*

Next-generation Micro-Exposure Tools (METs) with NA=0.5 (MET5) have been recently developed to demonstrate EUV patterning of features as small as 8 nm (half-pitch) [1]. The MET5 multilayer projection optics consist of a 2-mirror, modified Schwarzschild design and are subject to extremely stringent wavefront error and wavelength matching tolerances [2, 3]. To minimize wavefront error contributions in the MET5 system, the MET5 multilayer coatings were especially optimized to achieve simultaneously the highest reflectivity, lowest stress and lowest figure error. Multilayer coating stress values on the order of -100 MPa (compressive) were achieved, with peak reflectance around 60%. The multilayer coating profile in the lateral direction was designed for both M1 and M2 mirrors to produce a reflectance vs. wavelength curve with a phase and a centroid wavelength that remain constant at all locations within the mirror clear aperture, at the angles of incidence of the MET5 system. Multilayer thickness control across the curved surface of each mirror was achieved using a velocity modulation technique during deposition. The multilayer coatings for MET5 achieved non-compensable figure errors below 80 picometers rms, and an area-weighted centroid wavelength of 13.5 ± 0.05 nm, which was the specification for each MET5 mirror.

[1] M. Goldstein, R. Hudyma, P. Naulleau, and S. Wurm, "Extreme-ultraviolet microexposure tool at 0.5 NA for sub-16 nm lithography," Optics Letters **33**, 2995-2997 (2008).
[2] H. Glatzel, *et al*, "Projection optics for EUVL micro-field exposure tools with 0.5 NA", Proc. SPIE **9048**, 90481K (2014).
[3]L. Girard *et al*, "Fabrication of EUVL Micro-field Exposure Tools with 0.5 NA", Proc. SPIE/APOMA **9633** 96330V-1 (2015).

This work was performed under the auspices of the U.S. Department of Energy by Lawrence Livermore National Laboratory under Contract DE-AC52-07NA27344 and by the University of California Lawrence Berkeley National Laboratory under Contract No. DE-AC03-76F00098. Funding was provided by Zygo Corporation.

Presenting Author

P65

Realization of EBL2, an EUV exposure facility for EUV induced contamination research

Norbert Koster, Edwin te Sligte, Freek Molkenboer, Alex Deutz, Peter van der Walle, Pim Muilwijk, Wouter Mulckhuyse, Bastiaan Oostdijck, Christiaan Hollemans, Björn Nijland, Peter Kerkhof, Michel van Putten

TNO, Stieltjesweg 1, 2628 CK Delft, The Netherlands

TNO is realizing EUV Beamline 2 (EBL2), a facility to investigate the effects of EUV radiation on surfaces to enable future EUV HVM production. The facility will be accessible to all parties working in the EUV domain. In this facility samples can be exposed to EUV radiation under realistic environmental conditions and analyzed. The Sn-fueled EUV source and collector optics can deliver intensities at the sample up to an equivalent of 500 W at intermediate focus (IF), enabling research for future generation scanners and HVM production. EBL2 consists of a beamline, exposure chamber with integrated ellipsometer, XPS surface analysis capabilities and an automated sample handling system. For sample handling a dual pod interface is used enabling samples up to 152x152x20 mm, this includes reticles, reticles with pellicles and dedicated sample holders. The cleanliness of the sample handling is at such level that backside cleanliness requirements of reticles are met and re-entry into a scanner is permitted. The XPS is capable of handling reticles for analysis on the quality area after irradiation without breaking vacuum to ensure optimal surface sensitivity. We report on the final design of the system and progress on the ongoing build of the system and the surrounding facilities.

Presenting Author

Norbert Koster is Principal Scientist at TNO and has a bachelor degree in precision engineering. He has worked in vacuum technology and EUV lithography since 1992. Since 1999 he is employed at TNO as lead vacuum engineer and plasma scientist. As such he is involved in projects for EUV Lithography, plasma technology, contamination control, nuclear fusion (ITER) and ion beam lithography. His current topic of interest is contamination control for optical systems which use highly energetic particles like ions, electrons and photons. Presently he also involved in high throughput AFM metrology and the realization of a new EUV exposure facility (EBL2) in Delft for optics lifetime research. He is a member of the Dutch vacuum society NEVAC, the American Vacuum Society (AVS) and the International society for optics and photonics (SPIE).

P66

Atomic-scale investigations of formation and aging processes of EUV optics

Joost W.M. Frenken

Advanced Research Center for Nanolithography (ARCNL)
Science Park 110, 1098 XG, Amsterdam, The Netherlands

This talk will start with a brief introduction about ARCNL, a new public-private partnership between the Dutch funding agency FOM, the two universities in Amsterdam (UvA and VU), and the company ASML. ARCNL focuses on the fundamental physics behind current and future technologies for application in nanolithography, in particular for the semiconductor industry.

We employ scanning tunneling microscopy in ultrahigh vacuum to acquire *live* movies of the deposition of molybdenum and silicon for the production of MoSi multilayers for EUV optics. For this purpose, we have developed a dedicated STM system that can image a surface with atomic resolution, while the imaged part of the surface is receiving a low flux of either atoms, for deposition studies, or ions, for erosion studies. The STM-observations reveal the atomistic mechanisms at play and thus enable us to understand what limits the quality of the multilayers that are formed in these processes. Temperature-dependent STM-studies enable us to visualize some of the natural aging mechanisms of thin films.

Presenting Author

Prof.dr. Joost W.M. Frenken is the Director of the Advanced Research Center for Nanolithography (ARCNL) in Amsterdam. He is a Professor of Physics at the University of Amsterdam, the VU University Amsterdam and Leiden University and is a member of the Royal Academy of Arts and Sciences (KNAW) in The Netherlands. Frenken is specialized on the atomic-scale physics and chemistry of surfaces and interfaces and has developed dedicated scanning probe microscopy and other instrumentation for the investigation of surfaces under a wide range of harsh, practical circumstances, including high temperatures and catalytic conditions. He is also co-initiator of two spin-off companies.

P67

Diffractive Optics for EUV Applications

Ryan Miyakawa, Henry Wang, Weilun Chao, and Patrick Naulleau

Center for X-ray Optics, Lawrence Berkeley National Lab
1 Cyclotron Rd, Berkeley, CA 94720

As EUV lithography matures, there is a continued need for high quality EUV optics. Although multilayer-based reflective optics are the primary workhorse for imaging at EUV due to their high efficiency, diffractive elements such as zone plates can also play an important role in certain imaging and metrology applications. The SHARP microscope at LBL and the EMDRS microscope at Samsung are two recent examples of EUV defect review platforms that operate using zone plate optics.

Because zone plates are holograms, they can be programmed to support customized geometries and pupil functions with arbitrary amplitude and phase. This versatility makes zone plates well-suited for implementing non-conventional imaging conditions, such as Zernike phase contrast microscopy, differential image contrast, or wavefront encoding, without any major modifications to the imaging setup.

Current binary-amplitude zone plates have efficiency of around 10%, but there are ongoing efforts to develop Mo- or Ru-based phase zone plates with increased efficiency. Although zone plates cannot fully replace reflective optics, in many cases they can provide a versatile, cost-effective imaging solution at EUV.

Presenting Author

Dr. Ryan Miyakawa is a project scientist at the Center for X-ray Optics at LBNL where he worked for the past 5 years on the Berkeley MET and upcoming MET5. His interests include high-NA interferometry and novel wavefront sensing platforms.

P68

Fabrication of EUVL Micro-field Exposure Tools with 0.5 NA

Luc Girard[1], Lou Marchetti[1], Jim Kennon[2], Bob Kestner[2], Regina Soufli[3], Eric Gullickson[4]

[1]Zygo Corporation, Extreme Precision Optics (EPO), Richmond, CA 94806, USA
[2]Akumen Engineering, LLC. (former employees of Zygo EPO)
[3]Lawrence Livermore National Laboratory, 7000 East Avenue, Livermore, CA 94550
[4]Lawrence Berkeley National Laboratory, 1 Cyclotron Road, Berkeley, CA 94720

In support of the Extreme Ultraviolet Lithography (EUVL) roadmap, Zygo Corporation developed 13.5 nm, 0.5NA R&D photolithography tools with small fields. Those tools are referenced as micro-field exposure tools, or *METs*. Previous papers have focused on the design and theoretical performance and the fabrication and testing of the optical components.

In this paper, results from the completed projection optic box (PO, POB) systems are presented. The achieved single pass transmitted wave front (CA – 30 cycles/aperture) the systems was better than 0.25nm RMS at the center of the field and < 0.48nm RMS over the 30um x 200um field, less than half of the original specification. The flare, as calculated from the component roughness data, is less than the 5% specification. The paper includes a presentation of results from the component mirror metrology, the multilayer coatings, and the system metrology. To support the tight specifications, the component and system metrology tests required test repeatability better than 50pm. To achieve the high quality wave front, the optic mounts had to produce very small surface deformation. Also, the precision and stability of the alignment had to be controlled to a few tens of nanometers. The mirror motion is controlled by a hexapod system. Results of alignment convergence, wave front
error at the center of the field and over the field, as well as reproducibility are presented.

Presenting Author

P69

Multilayer EUV Optics with Integrated IR Suppression Gratings

Torsten Feigl[1], Marco Perske[1], Hagen Pauer[1], Tobias Fiedler[1], Uwe Zeitner[2], Robert Leitel[2], Hans-Christoph Eckstein[2], Philipp Schleicher[2], Sven Schröder[2], Marcus Trost[2], Stefan Risse[2], Christian Laubis[3], Frank Scholze[3]

1 optiX fab GmbH, Hans-Knöll-Str. 6, 07745 Jena, Germany
2 Fraunhofer IOF, Albert-Einstein-Str. 7, 07745 Jena, Germany
3 PTB Berlin, Abbestr. 2-12, 10587 Berlin, Germany

Today's EUV source concepts for EUV Lithography focus on laser-induced plasma generation using CO_2 lasers in combination with Sn droplets. Different approaches of CO_2 laser suppression have been discussed and realized in the past such as binary phase gratings and CO_2 AR coatings. While CO_2 AR coatings suffer from a significant EUV reflectance loss at 13.5 nm wavelength, binary phase gratings for 10.6 µm show great advantages in terms of EUV reflectance, IR suppression factors and mechanical stability. Binary grating structures for 10.6 µm are implemented in today's LPP collector mirrors. They significantly suppress the CO_2 laser wavelength of 10.6 µm and contribute to clean EUV photons in the intermediate focus. The paper focusses on different manufacturing approaches to realize multilayer EUV optics with integrated IR suppression gratings. Advantages and disadvantages of multilayer versus substrate structuring will be discussed and critically reviewed. The optical performance of a dual-wavelength spectral purity filter that combines two binary phase gratings optimized for 10.6 µm and 1064 nm will be shown. The dual-wavelength spectral purity filter can be used in future EUV collector mirror generations to suppress the pre- and main-pulse IR radiation.

Presenting Author

Torsten Feigl studied Physics at the Friedrich-Schiller-University in Jena, Germany and the Université Pierre et Marie Curie in Paris, France. He received his Diplomphysiker in 1995 and his Ph.D. in 2000 from the Friedrich-Schiller-University in Jena, Germany. Torsten Feigl joined the Fraunhofer IOF in 1994. For more than ten years he was leading the "EUV and soft X-ray optics" working group at IOF. In 2013 Torsten Feigl started to work as CEO of optiX fab, a Fraunhofer spin-off company. Located in Jena, Germany, optiX fab designs, develops and fabricates EUV imaging, illumination and collector optics. optiX fab is currently supplying chipmakers, EUV tool and source manufacturers as well as institutes, universities, synchrotron beamlines and EUV research consortia worldwide with customized multilayer and grazing incidence optics for EUV lithography applications at 13.5 nm and the entire XUV, soft and hard X-ray spectral range. Torsten Feigl is author of more than 50 EUV and X-ray optics related publications and patents.

P71

Modeling the Interaction of EUV radiation with Photoresist Materials

[1]Kristina D. Closser, [1]David Prendergast, [2]Musa Ahmed, [1]Paul D. Ashby, [2]Oleg Kostko, [1]D. Frank Ogletree, [1]Deirdre L . Olynick, [2]D. Slaughter, [2]Bo Xu, [3]Patrick Naulleau

[1]Molecular Foundry, Lawrence Berkeley National Laboratory
[2]Chemical Sciences Division, Lawrence Berkeley National Laboratory
[3]Center for X-ray Optics (CXRO), Lawrence Berkeley National Laboratory

The interaction of extreme ultraviolet radiation (EUV) with a photoresist, and subsequent decay of the resulting excitation dictates the efficacy of any scheme for EUV lithography. However, these fundamental processes remain poorly understood. The high energy (92 eV) photons associated with EUV may access additional pathways than those available to the current standard, lower energy DUV photons (6.4 eV). Ab initio calculations further our understanding of the interaction of EUV radiation with matter and offer new insights into designing novel, EUV-optimal photoresists. Computing the spectra associated with the initial optical absorption, and electron energy loss, provide a basic description of the electronic events that occur before the atoms in the resist have time to rearrange. The associated photoproducts can then be explored using the electronic forces and ab initio molecular dynamics.

EUV photons at 92 eV will ionize both valence and semi-core electrons, with a higher probability of interacting with the electrons in residing in semi-core states. These semi-core electronic states are generally localized on individual atoms, suggesting the potential for inducing selective photo-fragmentation of materials possessing elements which have high optical cross-sections at EUV energies. Recent progress in computing EUV excitations in model resist materials will be discussed.

Presenting Author

Kristina works at the Molecular Foundry at LBNL with David Prendergast. Her current research focuses on modeling the interaction of EUV radiation with photoresist materials at the atomic level. She received her Ph.D. from UC Berkeley with Martin Head-Gordon, where she developed new methodology for computing electronically excited states of large atomic and molecular clusters.

P72

EUV Radiation Chemistry Fundamentals: Novel Probing Techniques

Oleg Kostko, B. Xu, D. S. Slaughter, K. D. Closser, S. Bhattarai, B. Hinsberg, G. M. Wallraff, D. L. Olynick, D. G. Prendergast, P. D. Ashby, D. F. Ogletree, Y. Liu, P. Naulleau, M. Ahmed

Chemical Sciences Division, Lawrence Berkeley National Laboratory, 1 Cyclotron Rd, Berkley, CA 94720, USA

Tailored design of efficient photoresist is impossible without fundamental understanding of EUV induced chemistry. Resists incorporating high cross-section elements efficiently utilize EUV photons via radiation absorption by core-level electrons, resulting in emission of primary and secondary (Auger) electrons. Gas-phase mass spectrometry and photoelectron spectroscopy techniques reveal the response of individual prototype resist molecules to EUV radiation and electron collisions deciphering the energies of emitted primary and secondary electrons as well as fragmentation patterns. Quantitative information, such as electron yield per molecule, could be extracted as well. Dissociative electron attachment is studied to understand effect of thermalized electrons on intact resist molecules. While gas-phase studies do provide insight into the primary EUV induced events in the individual molecules, we seek to understand these processes in the condensed phase as this is where industrially relevant processes will occur. Aerosol techniques allow for generation of resist nanoparticles of different morphology. The nanoparticles are injected into the photoelectron spectrometer, which will demonstrate how the resist properties change in solid state.

Presenting Author

After graduation from the Brest State University, Belarus Oleg Kostko worked in the Institute of Solid State and Semiconductors Physics of the National Academy of Sciences of Belarus. He obtained his doctoral degree from the University of Freiburg, Germany in 2007 for study of gas-phase clusters by means of ultraviolet photoelectron spectroscopy. Same year he joined Chemical Sciences Division of the Lawrence Berkeley National Laboratory, USA as a postdoctoral fellow. He explored gas-phase and condensed molecules at the VUV beamline of the Advanced Light Source. After a short stay at SRI International, where he studied atmospherically relevant processes, he returned back to the Berkeley Lab to lead an effort for developing novel spectroscopies on nanoscale systems.

P73

Fundamental Aspect of Photosensitized Chemically Amplified Resist: How to overcome RLS trade-off

Seiichi Tagawa[1,2] and PSCAR Collaboration Members

[1]*Graduate School of Engineering, Osaka University, Ibaraki, Osaka 567-0047, Japan,*
[2]*Institute of Scientific and Industrial Research, Osaka University, Ibaraki, Osaka 567-0047, Japan*

Extreme ultraviolet (EUV) lithography is a leading candidate of the next generation lithography for a long time. However, high volume manufacturing (HVM) by EUV lithography is expected to start soon based on the recent progress in EUV technology. Especially improvement of EUV light source power has been carried out recently, although the EUV light intensity is not enough yet. The light source intensity and the resist sensitivity are complementary each other. It is necessary to increase the EUV resist sensitivity to compensate the low intensity of the EUV light source and also to reduce the cost of the development and the maintenance of high power EUV exposure systems. However, improving the resist sensitivity is challenging owing to two important problems faced in EUV/EB resists: [1] The most difficult technical requirement with regard to EUV resists is the simultaneous improvement in resolution, line edge roughness (LER), and sensitivity (so-called RLS trade-off)[1] and [2] the reaction mechanisms of the pattern formation processes change dramatically from photochemistry in KrF / ArF photoresists to radiation chemistry in EUV/EB resists, especially acid generation processes[2].

In the RLS trade-off, there are no fundamental differences in simulations for photoresists and EUV/EB resists after latent acid image formation[1]. However, the acid generation mechanism is very different between radiation chemistry and photochemistry[3]. The material design of CARs for ionizing radiation requires different knowledge based on not photochemistry but radiation chemistry. Therefore, a standard resist pattern formation model of EUV CARs including radiation chemistry based on a number of experimental and simulation works was proposed[2]. According to this approach, the performance of EUV resists has been improved very steadily year by year owing to worldwide efforts. However, the improvement of RLS trade-off based on the standard resist pattern formation model has become gradually slow. In this regards, it is problematic that the RLS trade-off of EUV resists has not been improved much in recent years.

Therefore, a very new process: high resist sensitization by the combination lithography of EUV or EB pattern exposure with UV flood exposure (PF combination lithography) of photosensitized chemically amplified resist (PS-CAR) was proposed[4]. The combination lithography of EB pattern exposure with UV flood exposure achieved a sensitivity enhancement without loss in space resolution[4]. Based on RLS trade-off simulation method[1], the breakthrough of RLS trade-off by PF combination lithography of PS-CAR is explained[4,5].

Postexposure delay (PED) effects suffered from airborne contamination in the PF combination lithography of PS-CAR were reported[6]. Recently more researches on *Photosensitized Chemically Amplified Resist*™, (PSCAR™) for EUVL HVM of semiconductor devices were presented[7,8,9,10,11].

In the present lecture, we talk shortly about the summary of early papers of photosensitized chemically amplified resist and then mainly about the fundamental aspect of the photosensitized chemically amplified resist.

REFERENCES

1. G.M. Gallatin, Proc. SPIE 5754, 38 (2005)
2. T. Kozawa, S. Tagawa, Jpn J. Appl. Phys. 49, 030001 (2010) and references in it
3. S. Tagawa, S. Nagahara, T. Iwamoto, M. Wakita, T. Kozawa, Y. Yamamoto, D. Werst, A. D. Trifunac, Proc. SPIE 3999, 204 (2000)
4. S. Tagawa, S. Enomoto, A. Oshima, "Super High Sensitivity Enhancement by Photo-Sensitized Chemically Amplified Resist (PS-CAR) Process," J. Photopoly. Sci. Tech. 26, 825 (2013).
5. Tagawa S., "Photosensitized chemically amplified extreme-UV/electron beam resist," SPIE Newsroom, 13 March 2014
6. Seiichi Tagawa, Akihiro Oshima, Satoshi Enomoto, C. Q. Dinh, "High-resist sensitization by pattern and flood combination lithography," Proc. SPIE 9048, 90481S (2014)
7. Seiichi Tagawa, Akihiro Oshima, Cong Que Dinh, Shigehiro Nishijima, Seiji nagahara, Michael Carcasi, Gosuke Shiraishi, Yuichi Terashita, Yukie Minekawa, Kosuke Yoshihara, Hisashi Nakagawa, Takehiko Naruoka, Tomoki Nagai, "The reaction mechanism and patterning of photosensitized chemically amplified resists", SPIE Advanced Lithography (2016)
8. Seiji Nagahara, Michael A. Carcasi, Gosuke Shiraishi, Yuichi Terashita, Yukie Minekawa, Kosuke Yoshihara, Masaru Tomono, Hironori Mizoguchi, Hideo Nakashima, Seiichi Tagawa, Akihiro Oshima, Hisashi Nakagawa, Takehiko Naruoka, Tomoki Nagai, Elizabeth Buitrago, Michaela Vockenhuber, Yasin Ekinci, Oktay Yildirim, Marieke Meeuwissen, Coen Verspaget, Rik Hoefnagels, Gijsbert Rispens, Raymond Maas, "Challenge toward breakage of RLS trade-off by new resists and processes for EUV lithography", SPIE Advanced Lithography (2016)
9. Tomoki Nagai, Hisashi Nakagawa, Takehiko Naruoka, Seiichi Tagawa, Akihiro Oshima, Seiji Nagahara, Gosuke Shiraishi, Yukie Minekawa, Yuichi Terashita, Kosuke Yoshihara, Elizabeth Buitrago, Michaela Vockenhuber, Yasin Ekinci, Oktay Yildirim, Marieke Meeuwissen, Rik Hoefnagels, Gijsbert Rispens, Coen Verspaget, Raymond Maas, "Novel high-sensitivity EUV photoresist for sub-7nm node", SPIE Advanced Lithography (2016)
10. Elizabeth Buitrago, Seiji Nagahara, Oktay Yildirim, Hisashi Nakagawa, Seiichi Tagawa, Marieke Meeuwissen, Tomoki Nagai, Takehiko Naruoka, Coen Verspaget, Rik Hoefnagels, Gijsbert Rispens, Gosuke Shiraishi, Yuichi Terashita, Yukie Minekawa, Kosuke Yoshihara, Akihiro Oshima, Michaela Vockenhuber, Yasin Ekinci, "Sensitivity enhancement of chemically amplified resist and evaluation using EUV interference lithography", SPIE Advanced Lithography (2016)
11. Seiichi Tagawa, Akihiro Oshima, Cong Que Dinh, Shigehiro Nishijima, "Fundamental aspects of a new process of high-resist sensitization by the combination lithography of EB/EUV pattern exposure with UV flood exposure of photosensitized CAR and non-CAR", SPIE Advanced Lithography (2016)

Presenting Author

P74

Molecular Resist Materials for Extreme Ultraviolet Lithography

Hiroki Yamamoto[1], Hiroto Kudo[2], and Takahiro Kozawa[1]

[1]The Institute of Scientific and Industrial Research, Osaka University, 8-1 Mihogaoka, Ibaraki, Osaka 567-0047, Japan (Osaka Univ.)

[2]Department of Chemistry and Materials Engineering, Faculty of Chemistry, Materials and Bioengineering, Kansai University, 3-3-35, Yamate-cho, Suita-shi, Osaka 564-8680, Japan

Owing to the world-wide efforts, the resolution of EUV lithography with chemically amplified resist processes has already reached sub-16 nm region. With the progress in the resolution, the feasibility of sub-10 nm half-pitch has, recently, attracted much attention from the viewpoint of the extendibility of EUV lithography. For the development of high resolution resist materials, the reduction of molecular size is inevitable. In this presentation, the development and potential of molecular resists are discussed.

Presenting Author

P75

Tin Cage Photoresists for EUV Lithography

Jarich Haitjema

Nano photochemistry Group, Advanced Research Center for Nanolithography (ARCNL), The Netherlands

Recently, organometallic photoresists have attracted attention because of their higher absorption of EUV light compared to organic materials. One of the metals with a high EUV absorption cross-section is tin (Sn). Higher absorption of EUV light can be favorable for the sensitivity of the photoresist. Additionally, a higher number of absorbed photons reduces stochastic effects, which is beneficial for reducing line edge roughness (LER). This work aims to provide insight in the EUV lithographic performance of an organometallic cage compound containing twelve Sn atoms. This cage compound was exposed to EUV light at the Paul Scherrer Institute, Switzerland. Although the compound performs as a negative resist, a decrease in the layer thickness was observed at higher doses, related to outgassing of organic compounds. This finding provides useful insights in the mechanism of organometallic photoresists. Understanding the chemical mechanism behind the solubility change is key for improving the photoresist performance. In our experiments, the pattern formation was significantly improved in comparison with previously published results for related compounds.

Presenting Author

Jarich Haitjema studied chemistry in Utrecht, the Netherlands, and continued his studies there with the master program "Chemistry and Physics". During his studies he has done research projects on catalysis (bachelor thesis project, supervisor: Prof. B.M. Weckhuysen), luminescence of rare earths (master thesis project, supervisor: Prof. A. Meijerink), and a short master internship at ARCNL which focused on metal-based molecular resist materials.

P76

Mechanisms of Exposure of Resists to EUV Light: Photons, Electrons and Holes

Amrit Narasimhan, Steven Grzeskowiak, Greg Denbeaux, Robert Brainard

SUNY Polytechnic Institute, Albany NY 12203

Absorption of EUV photons creates low-energy electrons (~80 eV). It is these electrons that cause most of the chemistry that occurs during the exposure of EUV resists. The mechanisms by which these electrons interact with resist components are key to optimizing the performance of EUV resists and EUV lithography as a whole. This presentation will focus on the specific chemical mechanisms of reactions between electrons and resists using experiments and modelling. Specifically, this presentation will have three parts:

(A) LESiS Monte Carlo Model: Comparison of Experiment and Model.

(B) Cross-Sections of EUV PAGs: Influence of Concentration, Electron Energy, and Structure.

(C) Internal Excitation in EUV Photoresists: E-Beam Induced Fluorescence.

(A)

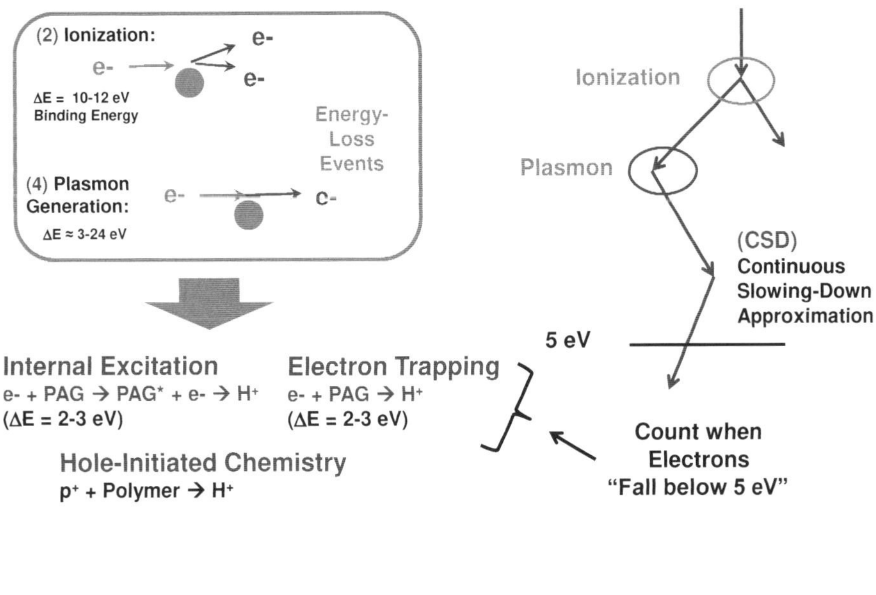

(B)

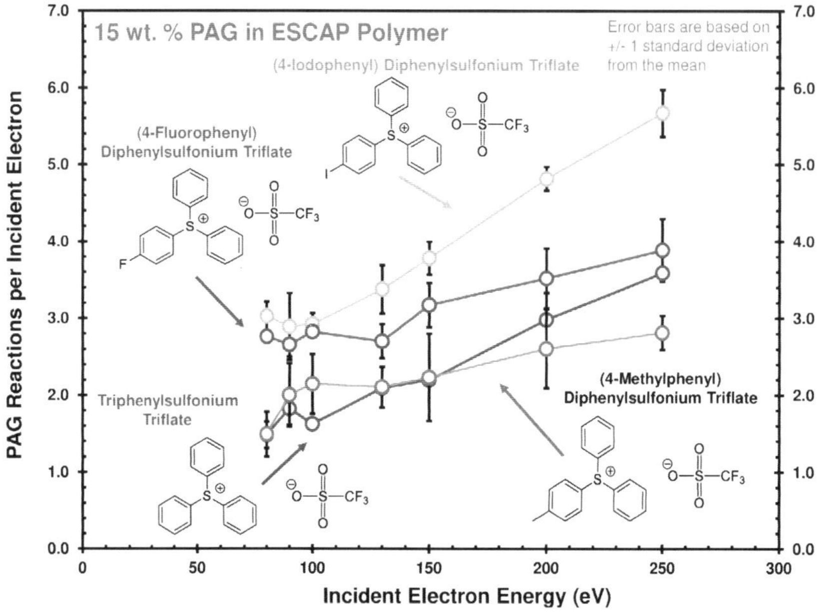

(C)

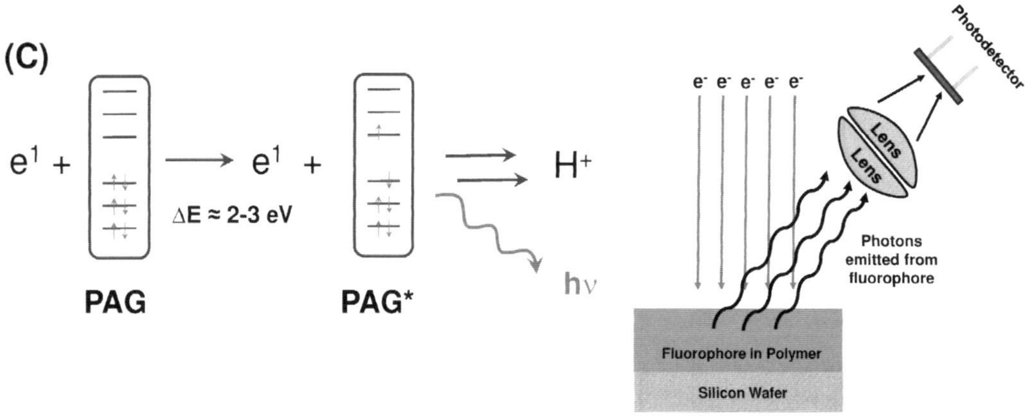

Presenting Author

P77

Advances in EUV Resists 2010-2016

Robert Brainard,[a] Gregg Gallatin,[b] and Mark Neisser[c]

a: SUNY Polytechnic Institute, b: Applied Math Solutions, LLC, c: Whitehouse Station, NJ

As EUV lithography becomes more of a reality, EUV photoresists have shown dramatic growth in sophistication, complexity and capability. This overview will present some of the best technical advances made by resist community in the past six years. Topics will include:

(1) Optical Density Goal Reversal:
- From "Need More Transparency" to "Need More Opacity" (Figure 1).

(2) The Physics of EUV Exposure Mechanisms:
- The Keys to Designing the Best Chemistry is Understanding the Physics

(3) Exciting New Resist Designs:
- Metal-Based Resists
- Nanoparticle Resists
- Molecular Glasses
- Dramatically New Photomechanisms

(4) Modelling of Resolution, LER and Sensitivity

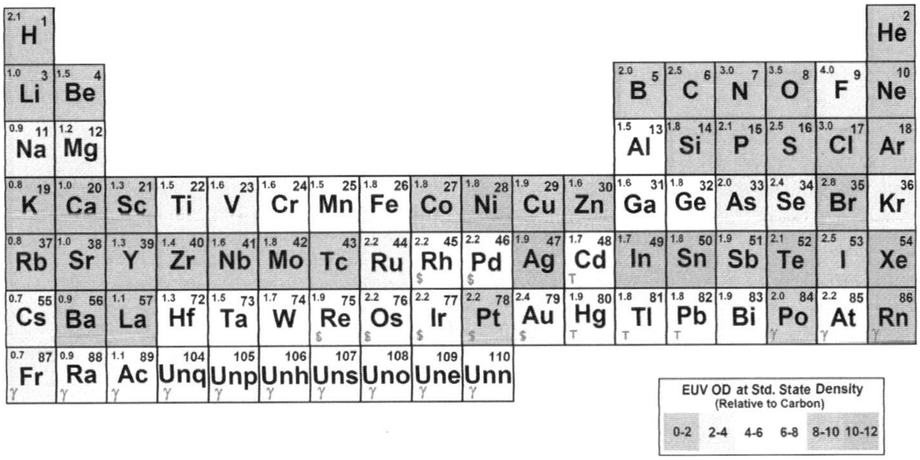

Figure 1. The periodic table color-coded by EUV optical density.‡

‡Cardineau, B.; Del Re, R.; Al-Mashat, H.; Marnell, M.; Vockenhuber, M.; Ekinci, Y.; Sarma, C.; Neisser, M.; Freedman, D. A.; Brainard, R. L. EUV resists based on tin-oxo clusters. Proc. SPIE 2014b, 9051, 90511B/12.

Presenting Author

P78

Fundamentals of X-Ray Excitation and Relaxation in EUV Resists

D. Frank Ogletree

Molecular Foundry, Materials Sciences Division, Lawrence Berkeley National Laboratory, 1 Cyclotron Road, Berkeley CA 94720 USA

Molecular relaxation is critically important for understanding and optimizing EUVL resist systems. The most strongly-bound molecular or atomic orbitals that can be excited by EUV x-rays have the highest photo-ionization probability. This means that the initial photoelectrons will have relatively low energy, and molecules will be left with a significant amount of residual internal energy. Relaxation generates additional secondary electrons, followed by molecular fragmentation into radicals and radical ions. Relaxation processes are especially important when resist sensitivity is increased by incorporating high EUV cross-section atoms, which promote the formation of strongly bound orbitals.

The challenge for resist designers will be to develop molecular systems that can harness this simultaneous localized explosion of chemical energy in the form of low energy electrons, radicals and ions for pattern generation. I will discuss experimental and theoretical investigations of fundamental EUV-resist interactions now being carried out by a multi-disciplinary team of LBNL scientists from the Molecular Foundry[1], the Chemical Dynamics Beamline[2] and the Center for X-Ray Optics[3].

[1] foundry.lbl.gov, Materials Sciences Division LBNL

[2] chemicaldynamics.lbl.gov, Chemical Sciences Division LBNL

[3] cxro.lbl.gov, Materials Sciences Division LBNL

Presenting Author

Dr. D. Frank Ogletree is a Staff Scientist and former Director of the Imaging and Manipulation of Nanostructures Facility at the Molecular Foundry in the Materials Sciences Division of the Lawrence Berkeley National Lab. He received his A.B. in Physics from the University of Chicago and Ph.D. in Physics from the University of California Berkeley, followed by postdoctoral work at LBNL. His research focus is on nanoscale materials characterization using electron and x-ray spectroscopy and scanning probe and electron spectro-microscopy.

P79

Metal Oxide EUV Photoresist for N7 Relevant Patterns

Stephen T. Meyers, Andrew Grenville

Inpria Corporation, 2001 NW Monroe Avenue, Corvallis, OR, USA 97330

Inpria is developing directly patternable, metal oxide hardmasks as robust, high-resolution photoresists for EUV lithography. Targeted formulations have achieved 13nm half-pitch resolution at 26mJ/cm^2 on an ASML NXE:3300B scanner. Newer formulations have achieved 16nm half-pitch with 4.2nm LWR at 18mJ/cm^2. Inpria's resist materials, based on a tin-oxide platform with extremely high absorbance (15-20/µm), are designed reduce the impact of photon shot noise at compared to conventional resists. These metal oxide resists have ~40:1 etch selectivity into a typical carbon underlayer, thereby enabling ultrathin 20nm resist films with minimal pattern collapse. In addition to updates on lithographic performance, we review further details on design considerations and introduce a model framework to describe the operating principles of this class of photoresists.

Figure 1: Example of resist patterning targeting N7 requirements, producing 16 nm HP lines at a) 24 mJ/cm^2 with a LWR of 3.6 nm, b) 18 mJ/cm^2 with a LWR of 4.2 nm, and c) 14 mJ/cm^2 with a LWR of 5.1 nm. Exposed on an NXE 3300 with dipole 60x illumination.

Presenting Author

Stephen Meyers is the Director of Resist Development at Inpria Corporation, a Corvallis, Oregon company pioneering the development of high-resolution metal oxide EUV photoresists. At Inpria he leads of a team of chemists in the design, synthesis and testing of new resist materials and related processes. He holds a Ph.D. in Inorganic Chemistry from Oregon State University.

P82

Challenges for Predictive EUV Mask Modeling

P. Evanschitzky, A. Erdmann

Fraunhofer IISB, Schottkystrasse 10, 91058 Erlangen, Germany

In extreme ultraviolet lithography the mask has to be regarded as an active optical element with a significant impact on the overall system performance. Details of the 3D mask geometry and materials are important and must be considered in the mask modeling. The important mask induced aberration-like effects have to be represented correctly. Therefore, an accurate simulation of the light diffracted by the mask is essential. We present an optimized RCWA based model for the fast rigorous electromagnetic field simulation of masks. Arbitrary geometries and materials in combination with high accuracy and short simulation times require several model extensions which are presented. Specific challenges of the rigorous EUV mask modeling like multilayer defects and simulation areas which are typically larger compared to the wavelength than in the DUV case are introduced. For the simulation of larger mask areas a decomposition and field stitching technique combined with the rigorous EMF simulation model is presented. For the fully rigorous simulation of multilayer defects a data base approach is proposed. Finally, an overview on typical application examples like the impact of multilayer defects and their repair, the fast simulation of larger mask areas and the analysis of mask induced aberration-like effects is given.

Presenting Author

Peter Evanschitzky studied electrical engineering at the Universitaet des Saarlandes, Germany. He received his PhD in the field of optical surface measurement techniques at the Technische Universitaet Muenchen, Germany. Since 2002, he has been a scientist at Fraunhofer IISB, Germany. His field of research includes the development of simulation models for optical systems, optical and EUV lithography simulation, and optics simulation. He is coauthor of the lithography simulator Dr.LiTHO.

P83

Parallel and Decomposition Method for EUV Mask Simulation

Xiangzhao Wang, Sikun Li, Heng Zhang, Xiaolei Liu, Zhongliang Li

Laboratory of Information Optics and Opto-electronic Technology, Shanghai Institute of Optics and Fine Mechanics, Chinese Academy of Sciences, Shanghai, China, 201800

Mask simulations are necessary tools for optimizing lithography process. Rigorous electromagnetic method (REM) for EUV mask simulation provides accurate spectrum but consumes large computing resources (time and memory) especially for 3D cases. Various Fast models have been proposed for efficient mask simulations. This paper proposes a fast simulation strategy based on parallel and decomposition techniques. First, a 3D mask is divided into different areas, then parallel simulations with additional decomposition for these areas are performed. Finally, simulated spectrum of all areas are integrated. Two different decomposition methods are considered: the vertical decomposition computes the absorber and multilayer separately with analytical methods, the horizontal one constructs the 3D spectrum by 2D rigorous simulations in a similar way to variable separation. Both methods are compared with rigorous simulation, the result shows apparent speed enhancement within allowed errors. Further applications that employ different decomposition methods depending on specific situations can achieve better results.

Presenting Author

Xiangzhao Wang received his BE degree in electric engineering from Dalian University of Technology, China, in 1982, and his ME and DrEng degrees in electric engineering from Niigata University, Japan, in 1992 and 1995, respectively. Now he is a professor at the Shanghai Institute of Optics and Fine Mechanics, Chinese Academy of Sciences. His research interests include lithography imaging theory and technology, information optoelectronics.

P84

Actinic Mask Inspection System Using Coherent Scattreometry Microscope

H.Kinoshita, T. Harada, Y. Nagata, T. Watanabe and K. Midorikawa

University of Hyogo, Japan

An EUV mask inspection system, called a coherent scatterometry microscope (CSM), has been developed, in which high-order harmonic generation (HHG) is employed to produce coherent 13.5 nm light. The HHG-CSM was used to inspect absorber pattern defects (missing holes, bridges) for the 22 nm node by the die-to-die method and was found to exhibit satisfactory performance.

The coherent scatterometry microscope based on X-ray diffraction theory can yield phase information that allows us to reconstruct a two-dimensional (2D) image of real space. Of particular note is that the phase in real space is also retrieved separately. The phase distribution of a 1 um square-size phase defect was also reconstructed, from which the phase value was quantitatively evaluated. The height of these phase defects was estimated to be 5 nm, which were equivalent to the measurement data of AFM. Furthermore, by focusing the incident beam, it succeeded in 3-dimentional image reconstructing finer phase defect. We confirmed the usefulness of this inspection method.

Presenting Author

P86

Inspection Efficiency Comparison between Phase Contrast and Dark Field Microscopy for EUV Actinic Blank Inspection

Yow-Gwo Wang*[a,b], Andy Neureuther[a,b], Patrick Naulleau[b]

[a]Department of Electrical Engineering and Computer Sciences, University of California, Berkeley, CA USA 94720; [b]Center for X-ray Optics, Lawrence Berkeley National Laboratory, Berkeley, CA USA 94720

In this paper, we will compare the native defect detection ability between phase contrast method and dark field method for EUV actinic blank inspection by simulation. To study the possibility of EUV actinic blank inspection tool to identify not just the phase-dominated multilayer defects, but also the amplitude defects and the defects with a combination of phase and amplitude behavior on EUV mask blanks. Defect signal-to-noise ratio (SNR) will be calculated with the consideration of photon noise, speckle noise induced by mask roughness, and camera noise from EUV CCD camera. Moreover, in order to show the impact of photon level and pixel size in the inspection system toward defect SNR, we are going to consider the impact of various photon levels and the difference between inspection and review mode. Inspection and review mode have different amount of magnification, which can affect the inspection time of each mode. The simulation result will indicate which method would be the preferable solution for inspection/review mode in order to detect various types of native defects. Also, the minimum photon level which provide sufficiently high defect SNR for each mode will be discussed. This can translate to the EUV source power requirement of the tool based on these two methods.

Presenting Author

Yow-Gwo Wang received his B.S. degree from department of Electrophysics, and the M.S. degree from Institute of Electro-Optical Engineering at National Chiao Tung University in 2009 and 2011 respectively. Currently he is a PhD candidate at UC Berkeley and also a graduate student researcher at Lawrence Berkeley National Laboratory under the guidance of Prof. Andy Neureuther and Dr. Patrick Naulleau. His research is focusing on design, fabrication, and testing of mask/lens concept for EUV aerial image monitoring and inspection.

P92

Study of Energy Delivery and Mean Free Path of Low Energy Electrons in EUV Resists

Suchit Bhattarai[a], Andrew R. Neureuther[a], Patrick P. Naulleau[b]

[a]Department of EECS, Univ. of California, Berkeley, CA, USA 94720

[b]Center for X-Ray Optics, Lawrence Berkeley National Laboratory, Berkeley, CA, USA 94720

In this paper, we assess the relative importance of secondary electrons of various energies in delivering energy in photoresist films, and also present a calculation of the inelastic mean free path of these electrons in resist films. The energy delivery capability of secondary electrons is measured by using a low energy electron microscope (LEEM) to directly pattern large area ($\sim 15\mu m$ x $20\mu m$) features with 15-80 eV electrons and by analyzing the resulting dissolution contrast curve data. Results show that in 40 to 80 eV regime the energy delivery scales roughly proportionally with electron energy. In 15 to 30 eV regime however, this linear energy scaling does not adequately explain the resist thickness loss data. Dose required to lower the resist thickness down to 20 nm is 2-5X larger for 15 eV electrons than for 20, 25 and 30 eV electrons. We calculate the energy dependent inelastic mean free path of secondary electrons by combining the dielectric model for electron scattering in thin films and the electron-phonon scattering mechanisms obtained from literature. We measure the optical properties of the resist in the 0-100 eV regime required for performing these calculations by using a combination of optical reflectometry and electron energy loss spectroscopy (EELS) techniques. Results show that the inelastic mean free path values at energies between 10 eV and 92 eV range between 2.8 nm and 0.6 nm respectively.

Presenting Author